BREAD COOKBOOK

50+ Most Delicious Bread Recipes for Perfect Homemade Bread

(Great Baking Recipes for Beginners, Bread Cookbook)

Christine Jarrell

Published by Alex Howard

© Christine Jarrell

All Rights Reserved

Bread Cookbook: 50+ Most Delicious Bread Recipes for Perfect Homemade Bread (Great Baking Recipes for Beginners, Bread Cookbook)

ISBN 978-1-990169-33-5

All rights reserved. No part of this guide may be reproduced in any form without permission in writing from the publisher except in the case of brief quotations embodied in critical articles or reviews.

Legal & Disclaimer

The information contained in this book is not designed to replace or take the place of any form of medicine or professional medical advice. The information in this book has been provided for educational and entertainment purposes only.

The information contained in this book has been compiled from sources deemed reliable, and it is accurate to the best of the Author's knowledge; however, the Author cannot guarantee its accuracy and validity and cannot be held liable for any errors or omissions. Changes are periodically made to this book. You must consult your doctor or get professional medical advice before using any of the suggested remedies, techniques, or information in this book.

Table of contents

PART 1 1

WHAT IS KETO BREAD? 2

WHAT DOES KETO MEAN? 3

WHAT HAPPENS WHEN A PERSON GOES ONTO A KETOGENIC DIET? 5

SUBSTITUTES FOR FLOUR IN KETO BAKING 7

WHAT DO GLUTEN AND STARCH DO IN THE BAKING PROCESS 8

LOW CARB SWEETENERS YOU CAN USE IN KETO BAKING 18

KETO BREAD RECIPES... 28

Keto Cloud Bread 29
Keto Flaxseed Bread 31
Keto Poppy Seed Bread 33
Keto Onion Bread 35
Keto Cheese And Onion Bread 37
Keto Flatbread 39
Keto Flatbread Matzo 41
Keto Pita Bread 43
Keto Naan Bread And Melted Garlic Butter 45
Keto Poori Bread 48
Keto Soft Seed Bread 51
Keto Coconut Flour Bread 54
Keto Almond Flour Bread 56
Keto Savory Bread 58
Keto Pumpkin Bread 60

KETO CAULIFLOWER BREAD 62
KETO WALNUT AND ZUCCHINI BREAD 65
KETO COCONUT FLOUR BREAD IN A MUG 67
KETO ALMOND FLOUR BLUEBERRY MUFFINS............................ 68
KETO AVOCADO CLOUD BREAD.. 70

PART 2.. 72

BASIC FRENCH BREAD.. 73
ITALIAN BREAD 76
POTATO BREAD.. 78
SWEET POTATO BREAD 81
BASIC WHEAT BREAD 84
WHOLE WHEAT BREAD... 86
RYE BREAD 89
BASIC ARTISAN BREAD 92
ZUCCHINI BREAD 95
PUMPKIN BREAD 97
PUMPKIN YEAST BREAD 99
WILD RICE BREAD 102
WHOLE WHEAT ZUCCHINI BREAD... 105
DATES & NUTS BREAD... 108
MUSHROOMS BREAD 111
POTATO MUSHROOM BREAD 114
OLIVE BREAD 117
STRAWBERRY NUT BREAD 119
PLUM BREAD 121
BANANA NUT BREAD 123
BANANA CHOCOLATE CHIP BREAD 125
BLUEBERRY CRUMBLE BREAD 127
CARROT WALNUT BREAD 130
ALMOND FLOUR BANANA BREAD 132

- ALMOND FLOUR COCONUT BREAD 134
- ALMOND FLOUR PUMPKIN BREAD 136
- COCONUT FLOUR BANANA BREAD 139
- COCONUT FLOUR PUMPKIN BREAD 141

Part 1

What Is Keto Bread?

The rules for eating a keto diet are quite restrictive when it comes to bread.

This is because a key part of the keto diet, is eating low amounts of carbs, and bread in general has a lot of carbs in it.

Traditionally made bread has too many carbs in it, to be a part of a keto diet.

Luckily there are a number of low carb bread recipes that you can eat as a substitute .

It is possible for you to make your own low carb keto breads, using ingredients such as...

- Almond flour
- Coconut flour
- Psyllium husk
- Cream cheese
- Eggs

This book contains 21 of the best keto friendly breads that you can make at home quickly and easily.

What Does Keto Mean?

A ketogenic or keto diet, involves eating low amounts of carbs. The reason for eating low amounts of carbs is because it can cause the body to burn more fat in a more efficient way.

How the keto diet got its name

As the glucose or sugar in your body are used up, your body will then switch over to burning stored fat as a fuel source instead.

When the body turns stored fat into fuel, it creates ketones. So the name keto actually comes from the first half of ketone.

To get your body to produce ketones, you can eat low amounts of carbs and a very small amount of protein. You need to eat lower protein, because your body is able to convert protein to blood sugar also.

A key role of your liver is to produce ketones from the stored fat on your body. Your body will only do this when there are no ready to access glucose in your blood stream.

The ketones that are produced by the liver can then be used as a fuel source by your body and brain.

Your brain is able to run very well on glucose or fat in the form of ketones.

What Happens When A Person Goes Onto A Ketogenic Diet?

When a person goes onto a ketogenic diet, their body will switch over to using stored fat as a fuel source. This will help to burn off excess body fat faster.

Eating a keto diet has a number of health and weight loss benefits including...

- Reduced feelings of hunger
- Weight loss
- A more consistent stream of energy throughout the day, which will allow you to be more focused and alert throughout your day
- More steady blood sugar levels
- Higher levels of energy and mental clarity (less brain fog)
- Stomach feeling clearer
- Higher levels of physical endurance

- In certain cases, a keto diet can reduce the amount of seizures an epileptic has

As your body begins to produce ketones, it will go into a metabolic state that is called ketosis.

A very fast way to get into ketosis is through fasting. This involves not eating any food. The only problem with this is that no one can fast for ever.

You can instead eat a keto diet, and that will put you into and then keep you in that state known as ketosis.

Doing this will then give you many of the benefits of fasting, including weight loss, with out having to actually fast.

Substitutes For Flour In Keto Baking

What are you trying to substitute for?

In normal full carb baking, the most important ingredients are...

- Gluten
- Starch

Gluten and starch are contained in the wheat flour used in the baking process.

Because you are baking keto bread, you will not be able to use wheat flour, and will need to add additional ingredients into your bread mixtures, that do similar jobs as gluten and starch.

What Do Gluten And Starch Do In The Baking Process...

Gluten

This is a type of protein in wheat flour. The gluten is responsible for the majority of the structure in bread baking or any other type of baking. High gluten flours also rise a lot higher, and brown more.

Starches

When you ferment bread, it's the starch that gets eaten up by the yeast.

A big problem for keto baking is that you can not use yeast in the baking process.

Because there is no food for the yeast to eat, there is nothing for it to ferment.

This means that you will not get a fluffy structure to your keto bread, that you would get in a yeast raised bread.

The ingredients you can use in keto baking, to replicate the jobs that the starches and gluten found in wheat flour normally do...

- Eggs
- Cream cheeses
- Psyllium husk fiber
- Almond flour
- Almond meal
- Coconut Flour
- Flex Meal
- Pumpkin Seed Meal

Eggs for keto baking

Eggs are great for making up for the lack of gluten in keto bread recipes. Gluten is one of the biggest contributors to the structure of non keto bread.

Eggs provide a lot of structure to keto bread, and can help to make up for the structure gluten would normally provide.

Eggs have great emulsifying properties, because of the egg yolk. This is good for keto bread baking because it helps to holed the batter or dough together. Also this will help to provide a bit more volume and texture to the keto breads you produce.

Cream cheeses for keto bread baking

This helps to add structure and chewiness to the keto breads you create.

Psyllium husk fiber for keto baking

Psyllium husk fiber can be used in keto breads where you want to get a more sourdough or rustic bread texture. This can be difficult to achieve if you are using eggs as the main thickener or stabilizer of the bread.

Psyllium husk is made from the husk of the Psyllium seed, which has been ground down into a powder.

When water is added and mixed in with the Psyllium husk fiber, it will gel up, instead of simply absorbing the water. This then produces a gel like substance.

If you add enough water, and then heat it up, it will take on an extremely elastic structure, just like gluten.

What is psyllium husk?

Psyllium can be sold in either whole psyllium form or a psyllium powder.

The whole psyllium husks are more effective for baking. However, if you can only get the psyllium husk powder, then simply use it in an equal volume as you would for the recipe if its using he whole psyllium husk.

Psyllium husk powder or whole psyllium husk can be used for gluten-free baking.

If you find it difficult to obtain psyllium husk at the shops, try looking in the health section.

Often it will be sold as a colon cleanser. This is because of its ability to absorb liquids.

You will be only using small amounts in the recipes so you will not be getting the full cleansing effect, unless you are consuming large amounts of bread made with psyllium husk in it.

Adding psyllium husk to your bread recipe will give your dough a thick, gooey consistency. This is the secret to great gluten-free breads.

Almond flour for keto baking

What is almond flour?

Almond flour is made out of almonds. It is a gluten free nut flour, and consists of nothing but ground up blanched (without skin) almonds.

Almond flour is most often used as a low carb substitute for wheat flour, when making keto breads and other baked goods.

How to use almond flour?

Almond flour is a very common ingredient that can be used in many kinds of baked goods.

Because almonds do not contain gluten, any dough you create with almond flour will not behave like traditional dough does.

Dough made with almond flour will not rise with yeast.

When you use almond flour in baking, you will need to add something to the recipe to absorb and bind the liquids.

The most common ingredients you can use for absorbing the liquids are...

- Ground psyllium husk powder
- Protein powder
- And/or eggs

To know the number of grams of carbs per 100 grams of almond flour, check the label on the almond flour you buy.

Almond meal for keto baking

Almond meal can be created out of whole or blanched almonds. Almond flour has a consistency similar to corn meal as opposed to wheat flour.

Almond flour can be used in the baking of items for a low carbohydrate diet. Almond flour will add moistness and a nutty taste to bread and other baked goods.

Coconut Flour for keto baking

Coconut flour can be used as an alternative to wheat flour.

It can be used by those on a low carb diet or those who are intolerant to gluten.

There are several health benefits to eating coconut flour including...

- Stabilizing blood sugar
- Improved digestion
- Better heart health
- Weight loss

What is coconut flour?

Coconut flour is created out of coconut flesh, which is dried and ground up.

Coconut flour originated in the Philippines as a by-product of the creation of coconut milk.

To manufacture coconut flour, coconuts are first broken open and then drained of all liquids.

Then the coconut meat is scraped out. Then the coconut meat is rinsed, grated and strained in order to separate out the solids from the milk.

The solids are then baked at a very low temperature till they dry.

Finally it is ground up into a flour.

The white coconut flour powder has a similar look to that of flour made from grains such as wheat. Coconut flour has a very mild coconut taste.

Coconut flour is a gluten free flour

Coconut flour is free from any gluten.

This makes coconut flour a good alternative for people who have

- Celiac disease

- Wheat allergy
- Non celiac gluten sensitivity

Benefits of eating coconut flour

Coconut flour can help to promote, stable blood sugar levels and also a healthier heart.

Additionally coconut flour can have antibacterial proprieties and may also aid digestion and weight loss.

Flex Meal for keto baking

Flex seeds are a very nutritious type of food.

One table spoon of whole flex seeds contains a high amount of healthy elements including...

- Omega-3 fatty acids
- Fiber
- Copper
- Magnesium
- Thiamin
- Manganese

Flex seeds that are ground up into flour are even more nutritionally dense. This is because they are in a easier form for your body to digest.

A great way to get more flax seed into your diet, is to use a flaxseed flour when you are creating baked goods.

Flax seed flour has a high concentration of oil, which means you can use it as a substitute for eggs or fat in some of the baked goods you produce.

Also flex seed flour is a good substitute for wheat flour.

You can use flex seed flour to create

- Breads
- Cookies
- Pancakes
- Cakes
- Muffins

Pumpkin Seed Meal for keto baking

Ground pumpkin seeds can add a gluten-free healthy boost to any keto bread you create.

Pumpkin seed meal is made out of ground up pumpkin seeds. Pumpkin seeds contain

many health boosting ingredients and are a rich source of...
- Antioxidants
- Iron
- Zink
- Magnesium

Pumpkin seed meal when used to make bread, creates a great tasting and highly nutritious bread.

Low Carb Sweeteners You Can Use In Keto Baking

One of the main pillars of a ketogenic diet is to avoid almost all sugars and carbs.

Keeping your carbs macros super low, is what allows your body to trigger ketosis and start rapidly burning fat as an energy source.

For those who are new to a low carb diet, it can be tricky to fight the sugar cravings. However it is possible to overcome the sugar cravings, all it involves is 2 to 3 weeks of committing to staying off sugar entirely.

After you have weaned yourself off sugar entirely, you may find yourself with an urge for something sweet from time to time.

There are a number of ketogenic friendly sweeteners you can use to add the sweet taste into foods you create.

The top 3 ketogenic friendly sweeteners are...

1) Stevia

2) Erythritol

3) Xylitol

The best sweeteners for a keto diet

It is best to stick with stevia and erythritol, or a blend of the two.

Both are naturally occurring and don't cause blood sugar or insulin spikes, and they have a nice flavor.

Some people do complain of a slight after taste when they use stevia or erythritol on there own.

But when combined together the after tastes of each can be cancelled out.

1) Stevia

Stevia comes from a herb which is more commonly known as the sugar leaf.

The extract version is nutrient free. Stevia has become popular with people on a keto diet, this is because it has sweet flavor, free from the detrimental effects of sugar.

Stevia sweeteners can come in a liquid or a crystal form, in many Supermarkets and natural food shops.

Studies on stevia have shown that stevia can reduce blood pressure, as well as lower blood glucose and insulin levels in diabetics.

Also animal testing of stevia, has shown that it has good results for producing anti-inflammatory effects.

Liquid stevia is raw powdered stevia, mixed with a solution that keeps it pure.

Powered stevia is often mixed with other sweeteners that can contain hidden carbs.

What is stevia exactly?

Stevia is a plant which is a member of the chrysanthemum family, and also a subgroup of the Asteraceae family (regweed family).

Stevia rebaudiana is the more official name for the plant.

The Stevia you can buy in shops is very different from the Stevia that you can grow yourself.

The Stevia sold in grocery stores, does not contain the whole of the Stevia leaf.

Instead they are made out of a highly refined Stevia leaf extract which is called rebaudioside A (Reb-A for short).

Rab-A is about 200 times sweeter than sugar.

Rab-A can come in a number of forms including...

- Powder
- Liquid
- Granulated

What benefits of using Stevia?

Stevia is what is known as a non nutritive sweetener. This means that it contains almost no calories.

This can be useful if you are trying to lose weight.

If you have diabetes, Stevia can help to keep blood sugar levels stable.

How to use Stevia as a sugar replacement?

It is possible to use Stevia as a sugar replacement.

One pinch of Stevia powder is the equivalent of one teaspoon of sugar.

Things Stevia can be added to include...
- Tea and coffee
- Sprinkled on cereal
- Sprinkled on a unsweetened yogurt
- Put in smoothies

Stevia can be used in baking but may give the baked products a liquorice aftertaste.

Depending on the brand of Stevia you are using, you will have to play around with how much to use to achieve the desired tastes you prefer.

Because Stevia is so much sweeter than sugar, you will need much less of it.

2) Erythritol

Erythritol is a sugar alcohol that can naturally be found in fruits and vegetables. The commercial versions are normally extracted from corn.

Erythritol is an appropriate sweetener for a keto diet, this is because it doesn't affect blood sugar or insulin levels, and contains very few calories.

Erythritol is a low calorie sweetener.

Some people say that Erythritol has all the good things about sugar without any of the negatives.

What is Erythritol?

Erythritol is what is known as a sugar alcohol.

Sugar alcohols are used by food producers to add a sweet flavor to the foods they produce.

Sugar alcohols have a molecular structure that allows them to stimulate the tongs sweet taste receptors.

3) Xylitol

Xylitol is also a sugar alcohol. Xylitol is not very nutrient dense and has a very similar taste to sugar.

Xylitol has also been found to help aid with dental health..

However, Xylitol has been closely linked to stomach discomfort in some people. And Xylitol is lethal for dogs.

Xylitol has a similar look and taste to sugar, but has less of the calories, and as a result will not raise blood sugar levels.

What is Xylitol?

Xylitol is what is known as a sugar alcohol.

Sugar alcohols have a chemical structure which allows them to stimulate the tongs taste receptors for sweetness in foods.

Xylitol can be found in tiny amounts in several fruits and vegetables, and is therefore classed as a natural sweetener.

The human body also produces small amounts as part of natural metabolism.

Xylitol is commonly used in things such as sugar free chewing gum, mints and diabetic friendly foods.

Xylitol is similar in sweetness to sugar but actually has 40 percent less calories.

Xylitol from a shop will appear as a white crystalline powder, similar to sugar.

Because Xylitol is a refined sweetener, it contains no vitamins, minerals or proteins. Therefore it provides only empty calories.

Xylitol can be produced from the birch tree and similar trees, as well as from a plant fiber known as xylan.

Because sugar alcohols are carbohydrates, most of them actually do not raise blood sugar levels and as a result are not counted as net carbs, which makes them useful sweeteners for producing low-carb products such as keto bread.

The alcohols that are part of sugar alcohols are very different to those that get you drunk. Therefore they are safe for people who do not want to consume alcohol.

Xylitol for improved dental health

The bacteria in your mouth that cause plaque build-up and tooth decay, can not eat Xylitol and therefore will starve. This can therefore help to reduce cavities and inflammatory gums.

Summery of keto sweeteners

With any sweetener product that is labeled low or no carb, it is still important to look at the ingredients on the packaging.

Your goal should be to purchase the purest sweetener, and avoid products that contain fillers like...

- Maltodextrin
- Dextrose
- Polydextrose

Because these can spike blood sugar and sometimes contain unnecessary carbs.

There are many products that claim to be sugar free, that actually contain ingredients that don't technically count as sugar, but still have a large glycemic index, such as Malatol.

GI = Glycemic Index

Each kind of sweetener usually contains some level of carbs and calories, and the ability to affect your blood sugar levels.

The Glycemic Index is a way to measuring how much a food will raise the blood sugar levels.

It is best to use sweeteners with the lowest GI.

Because of food labeling laws in the United States, a lot of products are permitted to calculate these additional ingredients out of the net carb counts, and can really add up as secret carbs.

Sweeteners to avoid when baking keto breads...

- Corn syrup
- White sugar
- Coconut sugar
- Fruit juice
- Maple syrup
- Honey
- Agave

Because they all contain very high levels of carbohydrates and high GI numbers and can spike the blood sugar levels and insulin.

Keto Bread Recipes...

This section of the book contains 20 delicious keto bread recipes.

Each recipe will tell you...

- How many servings it will produce
- Ingredients you will need
- Easy to follow step-by-step instructions for creating each of the keto bread recipes

Keto Cloud Bread

Number Of Servings
- This recipe will make 6 servings

Ingredients needed...
- 3 ounces of mascarpon
- 1/8 a tea spoon of sea salt
- 3 large sized eggs (separate yolks and whites)
- (optional) 1/8 a tea spoon of cream of tartar

Preparation Instructions

1) Preheat your oven to 149 degrees C (300 degrees F)

2) Put into a large bowl the egg whites and cream of tartar, and beat with an electric mixer, until stiff peaks begin to form.

3) Next in a second large sized bowl, place the egg yolks, mascarpone, and the sea salt, and mix together until the mixture is smooth.

4) Next fold the egg whites mixture in with the mascarpone mixture, using a spatula. As you are folding the two mixtures

together, ensure you don't brake down the air bubbles in the egg whites.

5) Next, line a baking tray with some parchment paper, and then grease the paper lightly.

6) Now scoop the mixture, into 6 circular discs on the parchment paper.

7) Bake for 25 to 35 minutes, or until golden.

Keto Flaxseed Bread

Number Of Servings
-This recipe will produce 10 servings
Ingredients needed...

- 5 eggs
- 1 table spoon of dried oregano
- 1 tea spoon of pink salt
- 2 cups of flax seed meal
- 1/3 a cup of avocado oil
- ½ a cup of water
- 1 table spoon of baking powder (gluten free)

Preparation Instructions

1) Preheat your oven to 350 F.

2) Line a 13 X 9 baking pan with parchment paper

3) Put the dry ingredients into a mixing bowl: baking powder, salt, flaxseed meal, oregano. Put to one side.

4) Put into the blender the eggs and the oil. And then blend for 30 seconds, until the mixture becomes frothy.

5) Pour the egg mixture into the bowl of the dry ingredients, and mix together well with a spatula. Also add the water and mix well. Allow this mixture to sit for about 5 minutes.

6) Pour the mixture into the baking pan that's been lined with baking paper.

7) Put into the oven for 20 minutes, or until the top becomes firm and golden.

8) Remove from oven, and allow to cool on a cooling rack.

9) Cut up the bread into 10 pieces, and enjoy

Additional Notes....

- You can keep this bread in the fridge for up to 4 days.
- This bread is freezer friendly, and tastes great when toasted and buttered.

Keto Poppy Seed Bread

Number Of Servings
- This recipe will produce 8 servings

Ingredients needed...
- 3 eggs
- 4 table spoons of chia seeds (or flax seed)
- 1 tea spoon of baking powder
- 1 tea spoon of salt
- 8 ounces of cottage cheese
- 1 table spoon of olive oil
- 4 table spoons of sun flour seeds
- 1 tea spoon of ground psyllium husk (powder)
- 1 table spoon of poppy seeds

Preparation Instructions

1) Put all the dry ingredients into a bowl and mix up well.

2) Now stir in to this mixture the eggs, oil, and cottage cheese, and mix together evenly.

3) Allow this mixture to sit for 15 minutes

4) Line a baking sheet with parchment paper.

5) Spread the mixture out of the bowl, onto the parchment lined baking sheet.

6) Bake in a preheated oven at 175 C (350 F) for 20 to 25 minutes.

7) Once baked, place onto a rack to dry. (without parchment paper)

8) Once dry, cut up into 8 servings, and add butter and any other desired toppings.

Additional notes...

- You can store in fridge for 4 days
- Freeze if you want to store for longer
- This bread tastes amazing toasted right out of the freezer with a little butter.

Keto Onion Bread

Number Of Servings
- This recipe will produce 15 slices of bread

Ingredients needed...
- 5 table spoons of coconut oil
- 1 table spoon of erythritol
- ½ tea spoon of sea salt
- ¾ a cup of coconut flour (that has been sifted)
- 6 large sized eggs
- ¼ a cup of (unsweetened) coconut milk
- 3 table spoons of organic onion flakes
- 1 tea spoon of baking powder

Preparation Instructions

1) Pre heat your oven to 175 C (350 F)

2) Brake the 5 eggs into a mixing bowl, and slightly beat them.

3) Add to the eggs in the mixing bowl, the coconut oil, coconut milk, onion flakes, lachanto, salt, and baking powder. And whisk all these ingredients together well.

4) Now add the coconut flour to this mixture.

5) Now, grease a loaf pan (sized 9x5x3 inch)

6) Pour the mixture into the greased loaf pan.

7) Bake the mixture for 40 to 45 minutes at 175 C (350 F)

8) Once baked, remove from the oven and allow to cool for 10 to 15 minutes. (Before removing from the loaf pan)

9) Cut slices when you need them

Keto Cheese And Onion Bread

Number Of Servings
- This recipe will produce 8 servings.

Ingredients needed…
- ½ tea spoon of yeast
- 2 whole eggs
- 3/4 a cup of only egg whites
- 2 table spoons of (grated) parmesan cheese
- Toppings (of your choice)
- 1 cup of shredded cheddar cheese
- 4 table spoons of warm water
- 1 cup of trim healthy mama baking blend
- 2 tea spoons of baking soda
- ½ a tea spoon of Italian seasoning
- ¼ a medium red onion, sliced into one inch pieces and sautéed

Preparation Instructions

1) Add to the warm water, the yeast and stir. Allow to sit as you prepare the rest of the recipe.

2) In a 8 inch skillet (that will fit into your oven) sauté the onions.

3) Put the sautéed onions in a bowl, and sit to one side for now.

4) Now in a large mixing bowl, mix together all the remaining ingredients. And allow to sit for 5 minutes. (This allows it time to thicken slightly)

5) Pour the batter into the pan and sprinkle with the onion and cheese.

6) Use your finger, to dimple the top of the batter slightly.

7) Sprinkle on any other seasoning.

8) Bake at 350 F (175 C) for about 30 minutes (until the top goes a light brown)

9) Remove from the oven, and allow to cool for 15 minutes.

Keto Flatbread

Number Of Servings
- This recipe will create one loaf of bread

Ingredients needed...
- 1 cup (100 g) of mozzarella cheese (shredded)
- 1 large sized egg (beaten)
- 2 (minced) cloves of garlic
- ½ a tea spoon of dried thyme
- 1 table spoon of cream cheese
- ¼ a cup (30 g) of almond flour
- ½ a tea spoon of dried oregano
- 1 tea spoon of fresh rosemary (minced)
- add salt and pepper to taste

Preparation Instructions

1) Combine in a medium sized bowl the mozzarella and cream cheese.

2) Microwave this mixture in 30 second intervals, stirring between each microwave session, until the cheese has fully melted and has formed a smooth

consistency. (Normally takes about one minute overall)

3) Allow the cheese to cool for a few minutes (to prevent the eggs from scrambling in the next step)

4) Now add to the bowl the egg, garlic, thyme, salt, pepper, almond flour, oregano, rosemary. And stir until well combined.

5) Pre heat your oven to 180 C (350 F).

6) While you wait for the oven to pre heat, line a baking tray with parchment paper.

7) Pour the mixture onto the baking tray, and flatten out into an even layer about ½ an inch thick.

8) Now bake for about 10 to 15 minutes, until the bread turns a golden brown.

9) You can serve this bread in a number of ways including, sliced into chips, cut up into bread sticks, top with a source and toppings of your choice, or use to create a pizza.

Keto Flatbread Matzo

Number Of Servings
- This will create one flat bread.

Ingredients needed...
- 3 table spoons of unsalted butter (cold)
- 2 table spoons of (ground) sage
- 2 tea spoons of salt
- ¼ a cup of almond flour
- 4 large sized eggs
- 3 table spoons of onion powder

Preparation Instructions

1) Pre heat your oven to 350 F

2) Separate the egg whites from the yolks

3) Whip the egg whites until they forms stiff peaks.

4) Mix to the whipped egg whites, the spices and half of the almond flour.

5) Add next, the butter (cut into bits), the egg yolks, and the other half of the almond flour. And mix together.

6) Spread the mixture on a baking tray, which has had parchment paper placed on it.

7) Bake for 10 – 12 minutes, at 350 F.

8) Then increase the heat to 400 F and cook for 4 to 5 more minutes.

9) Remove from oven, allow to cool.

10) Cut up into 8 pieces ready to serve.

Keto Pita Bread

Number Of Servings
- This recipe will produce 12 servings

Ingredients needed...
- ½ a cup (100 g) of almond flour
- 4 table spoons of coconut flour
- 1 table spoon of sesame seeds
- ½ a tea spoon of sea salt
- 1/3 a cup (60 g) of butter
- 50 ml of water (optional)
- 2 table spoons of psyllium powder
- 4 table spoons of flaxseed flour
- 1 tea spoon of dried rosemary (chopped or ground)
- 2 large sized eggs
- 4 table spoons of olive oil (extra virgin)

Preparation Instructions

1) Put all the dry ingredients in to a large sized mixing bowl, and mix all the dry ingredients together well.

2) In a pan melt the butter and mix in the olive oil.

3) Add the eggs to the pan and beat into the butter and oil, using a whisk.

4) Combine the dry and wet ingredients together in the mixing bowl. Then work into a dough with your hands. (Add sprinkles of water if the dough is too dry).

5) Next, put the dough into the freezer for about 10 minutes.

6) Next, brake off balls of dough, big enough to roll between two sheets of parchment paper, and turn into 5mm thick pita bread pieces.

7) Grill the pita bread (1 – 2 minutes each side)

8) If you would like crunchy pita bread, then grill for about 4 minutes (make sure not to grill too long to prevent burning).

Keto Naan Bread And Melted Garlic Butter

Number Of Servings

- This recipe will make 8 servings

Ingredients needed…

- 4 ounces of butter
- 2 minced garlic cloves
- 2 table spoons of ground psyllium husk powder
- ½ a tea spoon of baking powder
- 1/3 a cup of melted coconut oil
- coconut oil, Optional) for frying
- ¾ a cup of coconut flour
- ½ a tea spoon of onion powder (optional)
- 1 tea spoon of salt
- 2 cups of water (boiling)
- sea salt

Preparation Instructions

1) Put all the dry ingredients into a bowl, and mix well.

2) Now add to the mixture the oil and boiling water, and stir together well.

3) Allow the mixture to rise for 5 minutes.

4) The dough should turn firm very fast, and remain flexible.

If you have got the mixture right, the dough will resemble the consistency of play doh.

If the dough is too runny,, then add extra psyllium husk , until it has the right feel.

If the dough is too firm, then add some additional water.

5) Split the dough up into 6 to 8 even pieces.

6) Turn each piece of dough into a ball, and then flatten out with your hands on a piece of parchment paper.

7) Fry the nann in a skillet, over a medium heat, to the point when the naan turns a nice golden color.(add coconut oil so the naan bread doesn't stick)

8) In a pan, melt the butter, and add the freshly squeeze garlic.

9) Use a brush to apply the melted butter to the bread pieces, and lightly sprinkle the top with salt.

10) Pour the remaining garlic butter into a bowl, and dip bits of the bread into it.

Keto Poori Bread

Number Of Servings
- This recipe produces 6 servings

Ingredients needed...
- 1 cup of thick mozzarella (shredded)
- ¼ a tea spoon of baking powder
- 1 table spoon of almond flour (back up)
- ½ a cup of almond flour
- 1 ounce of cream cheese
- 1 egg

Preparation Instructions

1) Put into a mixing bowl the almond flour and the baking powder and mix well.

2) Next, add the mozzarella and cream cheese to the bowl also. And microwave the mixture for 1 minute (in 30 second intervals)

3) Now add the eggs and use a spatula to mix the melted mozzarella in with the other ingredients. (Before it cools down too much)

4) If the dough is too wet, add one table spoon of almond flour.

5) Roll the dough out between two sheets of parchment paper. (to about ¼ an inch thickness)

6) Next, use a ramekin (or small bowl) to cut the dough out into round pieces.

7) Lightly dust each round with a little bit of the almond flour.

8) Heat the oil of your choice in a frying pan

9) Test your oil temperature is ready, by dropping a small piece of the dough into the pan. When it sizzles and rises to the top of the oil, it is hot enough to use)

10) Now, drop a dough round (one at a time, into the oil in the pan. It should now rise to the top of the oil.

11) Now use a slotted spoon, to spoon some of the oil on to the top of the Poori, and make sure the bottom is not over cooked.

12) When the Poori puffs up and goes a golden brown, flip it over and allow the other side to brown also.

13) Once both sides are a light golden brown, then remove them from the oil

using the slotted spoon. And place them on a paper towel.

14) Allow to cool slightly, but serve warm for best taste.

Keto Soft Seed Bread

Number Of Servings
- This recipe will produce 20 servings.

Ingredients needed…
- ¾ a cup of coconut flour
- ½ a cup of flaxseed
- 3 tea spoons of baking powder
- 1 tea spoon of salt
- 7 ounces of cream cheese
- ¾ a cup of whipping cream (heavy)
- 1 cup of almond flour
- 5 and 1/3 a table spoon of sesame seeds
- ¼ a cup of ground psyllium husk (powder)
- 1 tea spoon of ground caraway seeds (or fennel seeds)
- 6 eggs
- ½ a cup of melted coconut oil (or butter)
- 1 table spoon of poppy (or sesame) seeds

Preparation Instructions

1) Remove the cream cheese from the fridge, and allow to come to room temperature. (so it will blend better)

2) Pre heat your oven to 175 C (350 F)

3) Put all the dry ingredients, (except for the poppy or sesame seeds, which will be used for topping the bread) into a mixing bowl. And mix together evenly.

4) In a second mixing bowl put all the remaining ingredients, and whisk until they form a smooth consistency.

5) Next, add the dry mix of ingredients in with the batter mix, and mix together well.

6) Now, place the dough into a greased bread pan. (4 x 7 inches).

7) Bake the bread for about 45 minutes, on the lowest shelf in the oven.

8) To know when fully cooked, prick the bread with a knife, when it comes out clean, it is done.

9) Remove from the oven and remove from the pan.

10) Remove the parchment paper, place on a rack and allow to cool.

11) Slice and add your favorite toppings.

Keto Coconut Flour Bread

Number Of Servings
- This recipe will produce 14 servings.

Ingredients needed...
- 1/3 a cup of olive oil (or coconut oil) (or butter)
- ½ a cup of coconut flour
- 2 table spoons of erythritol
- 1 tea spoon of xanthan gum
- 1 tea spoon of ground cinnamon
- 6 eggs
- 1/3 a cup of water (or a heavy cream) (or coconut milk)
- ½ a cup of ground flax seed
- 1 table spoon of baking powder
- ½ a tea spoon of salt

Preparation Instructions

1) Pre heat your oven to 375 F

2) Place into a food mixer (or blender) the eggs, milk or cream, oil and blend up until well combined.

3) Next, add the remaining ingredients to the blender, and mix together also.

4) Sprinkle the toasted sesame seeds on top of the loaf (if you desire).

5) Next, line a 8 x 4 loaf pan, with parchment paper.

6) Pour the batter into the loaf pan.

7) Bake for about 40 to 45 minutes, until a knife pricked in will come out clean)

8) Remove from oven and allow to cool on rack for 20 minutes.

9) Allow to cool completely before slicing.

10) Add toppings of your choice to each slice.

Keto Almond Flour Bread

Number Of Servings
- This recipe will produce 12 servings.

Ingredients needed...
- 2 egg whites
- 2 eggs
- ¼ a cup of butter (60 g) (melted)
- 1 and ½ a tea spoon of baking powder
- A pinch of salt
- 2 cups of almond flour (200 g)
- 4 table spoons of psyllium husk
- ½ a tea spoon of xanthan gum
- ½ a cup of warm water

Preparation Instructions

1) Pre heat your oven to 180 C (350 F)

2) Put 2 eggs and the egg whites from two eggs in a mixing bowl, and beat together (use the two remaining eggs to create mayonnaise if you desire).

3) Add the remaining ingredients into a mixing bowl also, and blend until you have a smooth dough. Be careful not to over

mix. 4) Pour dough into a small loaf pan (7 x 4 inches).

5) Bake for 45 minutes (until you can prick with knife and it comes out clean.)

Keto Savory Bread

Number Of Servings
- This recipe will produce about 3 medium sized loaves.
- 12 slices per loaf
- 36 slices in total

Ingredients needed...
- ¼ a cup of coconut flour
- 8 ounces of cream cheese
- 1 tea spoon of rosemary seasoning
- 2 table spoons of parsley seasoning
- 2 and ½ cups of almond flour
- ½ a cup of butter
- 8 whole eggs
- 1 tea spoon of sage seasoning
- 1 and ½ a tea spoon of baking powder

Preparation Instructions

1) Place into a medium sized mixing bowl, the butter and cream cheese, until it forms a smooth consistency.

2) Next, add to the mixture the sage, parsley seasoning, and whisk until fully mix together well.

3) Next add the eggs, and mix in also.

4) Now, add the flour and baking powder. And mix in also.

5) Next, grease 3 mid sized loaf pans.

6) Then, fill each loaf pan about half way with the batter.

7) Bake the bread for about 35 minutes, at 350 F.

8) When cooked well, it will have a golden brown color on top, and a knife pricked into the bread will come out clean.

9) Remove from oven and allow to cool.

10) Remove from loaf pans.

11) Slice and add your toppings of choice. (each loaf will procure 12 slices, depending on how thinly or thickly you slice your bread)

Keto Pumpkin Bread

Number Of Servings
- This recipe will produce 12 servings.

Ingredients needed...
- ½ a cup of coconut flour
- 2 tea spoons of pumpkin pie spice
- ¼ a sea spoon of sea salt
- 4 large eggs
- ¼ a cup of pumpkin seeds
- 2 cups of blanched almond flour
- ¾ a cup of erythritol
- 2 tea spoons of baking powder
- ¾ a cup of pumpkin puree
- 1/3 a cup of butter

Preparation Instructions

1) Pre heat your oven to 177 C (350 F)

2) Line a 9 x 5 inch loaf pan, with parchment paper.

3) Place into a large mixing bowl, the almond flour, erythritol, baking powder, coconut flour, pumpkin pie spice, sea salt. Mix all these ingredients together well.

4) Next, add to this mix, the pumpkin puree, eggs and the butter (melted). Mix all ingredients together well.

5) Pour the batter into the lined loaf pan.

6) Press down on the top of the batter to give it a smooth top.

7) Sprinkle the pumpkin seeds on the top of the loaf, and press in lightly.

8) Bake for 50 to 60 minutes.

9) When you can prick the loaf with a knife and it comes out clean, then it has finished baking.

10) Remove from the oven and place on rack and allow to cool completely before removing from the pan and slicing.

11) Add your favorite toppings to a slice and enjoy.

Keto Cauliflower Bread

Number Of Servings
- This recipe will produce one loaf of cauliflower bread.

Ingredients needed...
- ¼ a cup of psyllium husk
- ½ a tea spoon of baking soda
- 5 eggs (beaten)
- 2 cups of almond flour
- ½ a tea spoon of salt
- 1 cup of steamed cauliflower rice
- cooking spray

Ingredients for decoration...
- 1 tea spoon of pumpkin seeds
- 1 tea spoon of sun flower seeds
- 1 tea spoon of sesame seeds

Preparation Instructions

1) Preheat your oven to 350 F

2) Spray the sides and bottom of loaf pan with cooking spray.

3) Line the loaf pan with parchment paper.

4) Prepare the cauliflower rice (see later instructions)

5) Place into a large mixing bowl, the almond flour, salt, psyllium husk, and baking soda. And mix together well.

6) Next, fold the eggs and the cauliflower into the mixture. Mix the batter until it becomes smooth.

7) Pour the batter into the loaf pan and use a spatula to smooth out on top.

8) Sprinkle the top of the loaf with the sunflower seeds, pumpkin seeds, and the sesame seeds. Press down lightly into the loaf.

9) Bake the loaf for about 55 minutes, until the top of the bread becomes a golden brown.

10) Test the loaf is cooked properly, by piercing with a knife and when it comes out clean, its cooked well throughout.

11) When finished cooking, remove from the oven and allow to cool before removing from pan and slicing.

12) Slice and add toppings of your choice.

Instructions for creating cauliflower rice...

1) Wash the cauliflower thoroughly.

2) Remove any greens from the cauliflower, and cut up into 4 equal pieces.

3) Use the medium sized holes on a grater, to grate the cauliflower into rice like pieces. (Leave any large tough bits out)

4) Place the cauliflower rice pieces into a clean bowl.

5) Use a paper towel to press on the cauliflower rice, to remove any excess moisture.

6) Next, sauté the cauliflower rice, in a large skillet, on a medium heat, in one table spoon of olive oil. Cook but do not brown, until the cauliflower rice becomes tender. (About 5 to 8 minutes)

7) Use this cauliflower rice in the recipe as instructed above.

Keto Walnut And Zucchini Bread

Number Of Servings
- This recipe will produce one loaf

Ingredients needed...
- ½ a cup of butter
- 1 zucchini (grated)
- ½ a tea spoon of salt
- ½ a cup of coconut flour
- 6 eggs
- ½ a cup of walnuts (that have been coarsely chopped)
- 1 tea spoon of xantham gum

Preparation Instructions

1) Into a large mixing bowl, grate the zucchini.

2) Place all the other ingredients (except the walnuts) into the mixing bowl also. And mix with an electric mixer for 1 to 2 minutes.

3) Grease a loaf tray.

4) Put the ingredients into the loaf tray.

5) Level out the top of the loaf and place the walnuts evenly on the top of the loaf.

6) Bake for about 50 minutes at 180 C (350 F)

7) Remove from oven and allow to cool.

8) Once cooled remove from pan and slice.

9) Add toppings of your choice to a slice and enjoy.

Keto Coconut Flour Bread In A Mug

Number Of Servings
- This recipe will produce one serving

Ingredients needed…
- 1 table spoon of heavy whipping cream
- 1 egg
- salt to taste
- 2 table spoons of coconut flour
- 1 table spoon of olive oil
- ¼ tea spoon of baking powder

Preparation Instructions

1) Put all ingredients into a mixing bowl, and mix together well.

2) Pour into mug (mix all ingredients in mug to cut down on washing up).

3) Microwave for 90 seconds.

4) Remove from microwave and remove from mug.

5) Slice.

6) Add toppings of your choice and enjoy.

Keto Almond Flour Blueberry Muffins

Number Of Servings
- This recipe will produce 12 muffins.

Ingredients needed...
- ½ a cup of erythritol
- ¼ a tea spoon of sea salt
- 1/3 a cup of unsweetened almond milk
- ½ a tea spoon of vanilla extract
- 2 and ½ a cup of blanched almond flour
- 1 and ½ a tea spoon of gluten free baking powder#
- 1/3 a cup of coconut oil
- 3 large eggs
- ¾ a cup of blueberries

Preparation Instructions

1) Pre heat your oven to 177C (350F).

2) Next, Line a muffin pan with 12 parchment paper muffin liners.

3) Put into a large mixing bowl, the almond flour, baking powder, erythritol and sea salt. And stir together well.

4) Next, add to the mixture the coconut oil (melted), almond milk, vanilla extract and eggs. Mix together well.

5) Next, add the blueberries to the mixture, and fold in to the mixture.

6) Place an even amount of the batter into each of the 12 muffin cups.

7) Bake the muffins for about 20 to 25 minutes, until their tops become golden, and a knife piercing a muffin comes out clean

8) Remove from oven and allow to cool on a rack.

9) Eat and enjoy.

Keto Avocado Cloud Bread

Number Of Servings
- This recipe will produce 12 servings.

Ingredients needed...
- ¼ a tea spoon of cream of tartar
- a pinch of salt
- 4 eggs (separated)
- ½ a ripe avocado (mashed up)
- 2 tea spoons of toasted sesame seeds

Preparation Instructions

1) Pre heat your oven to 300 F.

2) Line a large sized baking tray with parchment paper.

3) Put into a large mixing bowl the egg whites and cream of tartar, and use a hand mixer to beat this mixture until it forms stiff peaks.

4) Place into a medium sized mixing bowl, the avocado, egg yolks and salt.

5) Use a hand mixer to mix these ingredients together until smooth.

6) Next fold in the egg whites mixture from the other bowl, until smooth and mixed well.

7) Use about ¼ a cup of the dough to create round and flattened pieces of bread. Spread out about an inche apartte on the baking tray.

8) Sprinkle each piece of bread with sesame seeds.

9) Bake for about 30 to 35 minutes, until golden and firm.

10) Remove from oven, and allow to cool.

11) Add toppings of your choice and enjoy.

Part 2

Basic French Bread

INGREDIENTS:

6 Cups Flour, all-purpose

2 ½ Cup Water, warm

2 ¼ Tablespoons Olive oil, cold pressed, unrefined

1 ½ teaspoons Sugar, cane, white

1 tablespoon Yeast, dry, active

2 teaspoons Salt, fine, sea

EQUIPMENT:

Stand mixer fitted with the dough hook, Small mixing bowl, Baking tray, Parchment paper, Cooling racks, Plastic wrap (optional).

PREPARATION:

Step 1: In a small mixing bowl add dry yeast and two tablespoons of warm water. Set aside on a countertop for 3-5 minutes to foam.

Step 2: Transfer the yeast water into a bowl of the stand mixer. Add salt, sugar, olive oil and half of the flour. Start mixing on medium-low speed and slowly add the rest of the flour. If the dough is sticking to the sides of the bowl, scrape it with a spatula. The dough will soon start forming a sturdy but soft ball.

Step 3: Leave the dough ball in the mixer and cover with a lid. Set aside for 10 minutes to rise. After 10 minutes beat with a dough hook for 30-45 seconds and set aside for another 10 minutes.

Repeat four more times.

Alternatively, you can leave the dough in the bowl, cover with a plastic wrap and set aside in a warm place for approximately one hour. The dough should double in size.

Step 4: Transfer the dough into a lightly floured surface. Knead it with hands for 1-2 minutes. Cut the dough in half. Shape each half into a loaf.

Step 5: Pre-heat the oven to 375°F. Line the baking tray with parchment paper. Place the loaves into the baking tray.

Bake at 375° for 30-35 minutes or until it becomes golden brown and baked through.

Transfer onto the cooling racks and let it cool.

Basic French Bread will keep for one week in a fridge or up to one month in a freezer.

Italian Bread

INGREDIENTS:

6 Cups Flour, all-purpose

2 ¼ Cup Water, warm

1 teaspoons Sugar, cane, white

1 ¼ tablespoon Yeast, dry, active

2 teaspoons Salt, fine, sea

EQUIPMENT:

Stand mixer fitted with the dough hook, Small mixing bowl, Baking tray, Kitchen knife, Parchment paper, Cooling racks, Plastic wrap (optional).

PREPARATION:

Step 1: In a small mixing bowl add dry yeast and two tablespoons of warm water. Set aside on a countertop for 3-5 minutes to foam.

Step 2: Transfer the yeast water into a bowl of the stand mixer. Add salt, sugar, and half of the flour. Start mixing on medium-low speed and slowly add the rest of the flour. If the dough is sticking to the sides of the bowl, scrape it with a spatula. The dough will soon start forming a sturdy but soft ball.

Step 3: Leave the dough in the bowl, cover with a plastic wrap and set aside in a warm place for approximately one hour. The dough should double in size.

Step 4: Transfer the dough into a lightly floured surface. Knead it with hands for 1-2 minutes. Cut the dough in half. Shape each half into a loaf. Make four shallow slashes on the top of each loaf with a kitchen knife.

Step 5: Pre-heat the oven to 375°F. Line the baking tray with parchment paper. Place the loaves into the baking tray.

Bake at 375° for 30-35 minutes or until it becomes golden brown and baked through.

Transfer onto the cooling racks and let it cool.

Italian Bread will keep for one week in a fridge or up to one month in a freezer.

Potato Bread

INGREDIENTS:

5 Cups Flour, all-purpose

12 Oz Potato, boiled

2 ½ Cup Milk, warm

2 ¼ Tablespoons Olive oil, cold pressed, unrefined

1 ½ teaspoons Sugar, cane, white

1 ¼ tablespoon Yeast, dry, active

2 teaspoons Salt, fine, sea

EQUIPMENT:

Stand mixer fitted with the dough hook, Small and medium mixing bowls, Potato masher, Whisk, Plastic wrap. Two loaf baking trays, Cooling racks.

PREPARATION:

Step 1: In a small mixing bowl add dry yeast and two tablespoons of warm milk. Set aside on a countertop for 3-5 minutes to foam.

Remove skin from the boiled potato. Place the skinned potato into a medium mixing bowl and mash with a masher. Whisk in warm milk.

Add salt, yeast, olive oil, and sugar. Whisk to incorporate.

Whisk in two cups of flour.

Step 2: Transfer the mixture into the bowl of a stand mixer. Start mixing on medium-low speed and slowly add the rest of the flour. If the dough is sticking to the sides of the bowl, scrape it with a spatula. The dough will soon start forming a sturdy but soft ball.

Step 3: Leave the dough in the bowl, cover with a plastic wrap and set aside in a warm place for approximately two hours. The dough should at least double in size.

Step 4: Transfer the dough into lightly floured surface. Knead the dough with hands for 1-2 minutes.

Cut the dough in half. Shape each half into a loaf. Place the loaves into two greased baking trays. Push down with your fingers. Set aside, cover with a plastic wrap and let the dough rise again.

Step 5: Pre-heat the oven to 350°F. Place the loaf trays into the oven.

Bake at 350° for 30-35 minutes or until it becomes golden brown and baked through.

Transfer onto the cooling racks and let it cool.

Potato Bread will keep for one week in a fridge or up to one month in a freezer.

Sweet Potato Bread

INGREDIENTS:

5 Cups Flour, all-purpose

12 Oz Sweet potato, boiled

2 ½ Cup Milk, warm

1 Cup Pistachios, chopped

½ Cup Cranberries, dried

½ Cup Raisins, golden, dried

2 ¼ Tablespoons Olive oil, cold pressed, unrefined

1 ½ teaspoons Sugar, cane, white

1 ¼ tablespoon Yeast, dry, active

2 teaspoons Salt, fine, sea

¼ teaspoon Cinnamon, powder

EQUIPMENT:

Stand mixer fitted with the dough hook, Small and medium mixing bowls, Potato masher, Whisk, Plastic wrap, Two loaf baking trays, Cooling racks.

PREPARATION:

Step 1: In a small mixing bowl add dry yeast and two tablespoons of warm milk. Set aside on a countertop for 3-5 minutes to foam.

Remove skin from the boiled sweet potatoes. Place the skinned potatoes into a medium mixing bowl and mash with a masher. Whisk in warm milk.

Add salt, yeast, olive oil, cinnamon, and sugar. Whisk to incorporate.

Whisk in two cups of flour, pistachios, raisins, and cranberries.

Step 2: Transfer the mixture into the bowl of a stand mixer. Start mixing on medium-low speed and slowly add the rest of the flour. If the dough is sticking to the sides of the bowl, scrape it with a spatula. The dough will soon start forming a sturdy but soft ball.

Step 3: Leave the dough in the bowl, cover with a plastic wrap and set aside in a warm place for approximately two hours. The dough should at least double in size.

Step 4: Transfer the dough into lightly floured surface. Knead the dough with hands for 1-2 minutes.

Cut the dough in half. Shape each half into a loaf. Place the loaves into two greased baking trays. Push down with your fingers. Set aside, cover with a plastic wrap and let the dough rise again.

Step 5: Pre-heat the oven to 360°F. Place the loaf trays into the oven.

Bake at 360° for 30-35 minutes or until it becomes golden brown and baked through.

Transfer onto the cooling racks and let it cool.

Sweet Potato Bread will keep for one week in a fridge or up to one month in a freeze

Basic Wheat Bread

INGREDIENTS:

3 Cups Flour, all-purpose

3 Cups Flour, whole wheat

2 Tablespoons Butter, melted, unsalted

1 ½ Cup Molasses

1 ¼ tablespoon Yeast, dry, active

2 teaspoons Salt, fine, sea

EQUIPMENT:

Large and medium mixing bowls, Spatula, Two loaf baking trays, Plastic wrap, Cooling racks.

PREPARATION:

Step 1: In a large bowl combine warm water, yeast and ½ of molasses. Mix in all all-purpose flour. Set aside for 30-40 minutes or until it becomes bubbly.

Step 2: Once the mixture becomes bubbly, add the rest of molasses, melted butter, salt and wheat flour. Mix with hands.

Step 3: Transfer the batter onto floured surface. Knead the batter with hands until it becomes firm but still sticky. You may need to add more wheat flour to get to the desired consistency.

Step 4: Place into a greased bowl. Cover with a plastic wrap. Set aside for 1-2 hours to rise.

Step 5: Preheat the oven to 355°F. Grease the loaf baking trays.

Distribute the batter between two greased trays. Bake for 25 - 30 minutes at 355°F or until the wooden tester comes out clean.

Transfer onto the cooling racks and let it cool.

Whole Wheat Bread will keep for one week in a fridge or up to one month in a freezer.

Whole Wheat Bread

INGREDIENTS:

6 Cups Flour, wheat

2 ½ Cup Water, warm

½ Cup Milk, dried, non-fat

2 ¼ Tablespoons Olive oil, cold pressed, unrefined

2 Tablespoons Molasses

1 tablespoon Yeast, dry, active

2 teaspoons Salt, fine, sea

EQUIPMENT:

Stand mixer fitted with the dough hook, Small mixing bowl, Baking tray, Parchment paper, Cooling racks, Plastic wrap Two loaf baking trays, Cooling racks.

PREPARATION:

Step 1: In a small mixing bowl add dry yeast and two tablespoons of warm water. Set aside on a countertop for 3-5 minutes to foam.

Step 2: Transfer the yeast water into a bowl of the stand mixer. Add salt, dried milk, olive oil, molasses, and half of the flour. Start mixing on medium-low speed and slowly add the rest of the flour. If the dough is sticking to the sides of the bowl, scrape it with a spatula. The dough will soon start forming a sturdy but soft ball.

Step 3: Leave the dough in the bowl, cover with a plastic wrap and set aside in a warm place for approximately one to two hours, depending on temperature in your kitchen. The dough should increase in size.

Step 4: Transfer the dough into a lightly floured surface. Knead it with hands for 1-2 minutes. Cut the dough in half. Shape each half into a loaf.

Place the loafs into the baking trays. Cover the trays with plastic wrap and set aside to rise for one to two hours.

Step 5: Pre-heat the oven to 350°F. Place the trays into the oven.

Bake at 350° for 35-40 minutes or until it becomes golden brown and baked through.

Transfer onto the cooling racks and let it cool.

Whole Wheat Bread will keep for one week in a fridge or up to one month in a freezer.

Rye Bread

INGREDIENTS:

2 Cups Flour, all-purpose

2 Cups Rye flour

1 Cup Water, warm

2 ¼ Tablespoons Olive oil, cold pressed, unrefined

½ Cup Sugar, brown

½ Cup Molasses

1 teaspoons Sugar, cane, white

1 ½ Tablespoon Yeast, dry, active

2 teaspoons Salt, fine, sea

1 teaspoon Anise, seeds, dried

EQUIPMENT:

Stand mixer fitted with the dough hook, Medium and large mixing bowls, (Pizza) Baking stone, Cooling racks, Plastic wrap (optional).

PREPARATION:

Step 1: In a large mixing bowl, combine flour, rye flour, sugar, brown sugar, yeast, anise, and salt. Mix with a spatula to combine. Add water, olive oil, molasses and mix with the spatula to incorporate. Cover the bowl with a plastic wrap and set aside at room temperature for 1-2 hours to rise.

Step 2: After the dough has risen, transfer it onto work surface dusted with flour. Knead the dough for 1-2 minutes, fold the dough in half, and then roll it into a ball.

Step 3: Generously sprinkle the bottom of a medium mixing bowl with flour. Place the dough ball into the mixing bowl and cover it with a plastic wrap. Set it aside for two hour to rise.

Step 4: Transfer the dough into a lightly floured surface. Knead it with hands for 1-2 minutes. Cut the dough in half. Shape each half into a loaf. Cut several parallel lines on top.

Step 5: Place the baking stone into the cold oven. Pre-heat the oven and the baking stone to 375°F. Place the loaves into the baking stone.

Bake at 375° for 30-35 minutes or until it becomes golden brown and baked through.

Transfer onto the cooling racks and let it cool.

Olive Bread will keep for one week in a fridge or up to one month in a freezer.

Basic Artisan Bread

INGREDIENTS:

6 Cups Flour, all-purpose

2 ½ Cup Water, warm

2 ¼ Tablespoons Olive oil, cold pressed, unrefined

1 ½ teaspoons Sugar, cane, white

1 tablespoon Yeast, dry, active

2 teaspoons Salt, fine, sea

1 teaspoon Rosemary, dried

1 teaspoon Sage, dried

EQUIPMENT:

Stand mixer fitted with the dough hook, Medium and large mixing bowls, Dutch oven, Heat-proof gloves, Parchment paper, Cooling racks, Plastic wrap (optional).

PREPARATION:

Step 1: In a large mixing bowl, combine flour, yeast, herbs, and salt. Mix with a spatula to combine. Add water and mix with the spatula to incorporate. Cover the bowl with a plastic wrap and set aside at room temperature overnight or up to 24 hours.

Step 2: After the dough has risen, transfer it onto work surface dusted with flour. Knead the dough for 1-2 minutes, fold the dough in half, and then roll it into a ball.

Step 3: Generously sprinkle the bottom of a medium mixing bowl with flour. Place the dough ball into the mixing bowl and cover it with a plastic wrap. Set it aside for two hour to rise.

Step 4: Preheat the oven to 425°F. Place the Dutch oven and the lead into the oven to preheat.

Step 5: Remove the Dutch oven from the oven, using the heat-proof gloves. Careful, it will be very hot.

Place the dough ball in to the hot Dutch oven, cover with the lid and place back into the oven.

Bake for 30 minutes. Remove the lid and bake for another 15 minutes until the crust will turn golden brown.

Step 6: Once ready, remove from the Dutch oven, transfer into cooling racks and let to cool completely.

Basic Artisan Bread will keep for one week in a fridge or up to one month in a freezer.

Zucchini Bread

INGREDIENTS:

3 Cups Flour, all-purpose

3 Cups Zucchini, grated

2 Eggs, large

2 ¼ Tablespoons Olive oil, cold pressed, unrefined

1 ½ Cup Sugar, cane, white

1 Cup Pecans, chopped

2 teaspoons Salt, fine, sea

1 teaspoon Baking powder

1 teaspoon Vanilla, extract, pure

¼ teaspoon Cinnamon, powder

EQUIPMENT:

Large and medium mixing bowls, Grater, Whisk, Spatula, Two loaf baking trays, Cooling racks.

PREPARATION:

Step 1: Preheat the oven to 355°F. Grease the loaf baking trays. Drain the excess water from zucchinis.

Step 2: In a medium mixing bowl combine all dry ingredients: flour, sugar, pecans, salt, baking powder and cinnamon. Whisk together.

Step 3: In a large mixing bowl combine all wet ingredients: zucchinis, eggs, olive oil, and vanilla. Whisk together.

Step 4: Combine dry and wet ingredients in the large bowl. Fold in with a spatula to incorporate all together.

Step 5: Distribute the batter between two greased trays. Bake for 45-50 minutes at 355°F or until the wooden tester comes out clean.

Transfer onto the cooling racks and let it cool.

Zucchini Bread will keep for one week in a fridge or up to one month in a freezer.

Pumpkin Bread

INGREDIENTS:

3 Cups Flour, all-purpose

3 Cups Pumpkin, cubed

2 Eggs, large

2 ¼ Tablespoons Olive oil, cold pressed, unrefined

2 Cups Molasses

1 Cup Pistachios, chopped

1 Cup Cranberries, dried

2 teaspoons Salt, fine, sea

1 teaspoon Baking powder

1 teaspoon Vanilla, extract, pure

¼ teaspoon Cinnamon, powder

¼ teaspoon Nutmeg, powder

EQUIPMENT:

Medium saucepan, Masher, Large, medium, and small mixing bowls, Grater, Whisk, Spatula, Two loaf baking trays, Cooling racks.

PREPARATION:

Step 1: Place pumpkin into medium saucepan and boil it until it becomes soft. Once the pumpkin is ready, place it in a small mixing bowl and mash it with a masher.

Step 2: Preheat the oven to 355°F. Grease the loaf baking trays.

Step 3: In a medium mixing bowl combine all dry ingredients: flour, pistachios, cranberry, salt, baking powder, nutmeg, and cinnamon. Whisk together.

Step 4: In a large mixing bowl combine all wet ingredients: pumpkin, molasses, eggs, olive oil, and vanilla. Whisk together.

Step 5: Combine dry and wet ingredients in the large bowl. Fold in with a spatula to incorporate all together.

Step 6: Distribute the batter between two greased trays. Bake for 45-50 minutes at 355°F or until the wooden tester comes out clean.

Transfer onto the cooling racks and let it cool.

Pumpkin Bread will keep for one week in a fridge or up to one month in a freezer.

Pumpkin Yeast Bread

INGREDIENTS:

6 Cups Flour, all-purpose

2 Cups Pumpkin, pureed

2 Eggs, large

½ Cup Milk, warm

2 ¼ Tablespoons Olive oil, cold pressed, unrefined

1 Cup Molasses

2 tablespoon Yeast, dry, active

2 teaspoons Salt, fine, sea

½ teaspoon Cinnamon, powder

EQUIPMENT:

Stand mixer fitted with the dough hook, Masher, Small mixing bowl, Baking tray, Parchment paper, Cooling racks, Plastic wrap.

PREPARATION:

Step 1: In a small mixing bowl add dry yeast and warm milk. Set aside on a countertop for 3-5 minutes to foam.

Boil and puree pumpkin with a masher.

Step 2: Transfer the yeast milk into a bowl of the stand mixer. Add pureed pumpkin, molasses, eggs, olive oil and half of the flour. Start mixing on medium-low speed and slowly add the rest of the flour. If the dough is sticking to the sides of the bowl, scrape it with a spatula. The dough will soon start forming a sturdy but soft ball.

Step 3: Leave the dough in the bowl, cover with a plastic wrap and set aside in a warm place for approximately one hour. The dough should double in size.

Step 4: Transfer the dough into a lightly floured surface. Knead it with hands for 1-2 minutes. Cut the dough in half. Shape each half into a loaf.

Step 5: Preheat the oven to 355°F. Grease the loaf baking trays.

Distribute the batter between two greased trays. Bake for 40-45 minutes Transfer onto the cooling racks and let it cool.

Pumpkin Yeast Bread will keep for one week in a fridge or up to one month in a freezer.

Wild Rice Bread

INGREDIENTS:
3 Cups Bread flour, unbleached
1 Cup Flour, whole wheat
2 Cups Rice, wild, cooked
½ Cup Sourdough starter, ripe
1 ½ Cup Water, warm
1 Cup Pistachios, chopped
1 Cup Cranberries, dried
1 ¼ tablespoon Yeast, dry, active
1 ½ teaspoons Maple syrup
2 teaspoons Salt, fine, sea
EQUIPMENT:
Stand mixer fitted with the paddle attachment and dough hook, Large mixing bowl, Plastic wrap. Two loaf baking trays, Cooling racks.
PREPARATION:
Step 1: In a bowl of a stand mixer add sourdough starter, water, yeast, maple syrup and whole wheat flour. Beat with the paddle attachment until smooth. Cover the bowl with a plastic wrap and let

it sit for 1 – 2 hours until the dough becomes bubbly.

Step 2: Add salt and gradually beat in the bread flour. Remove the paddle attachment and install a dough hook.

Knead for 8-10 minutes. Add rice, pistachios, and cranberries. Knead to incorporate.

Step 3: Transfer the dough into a large bowl sprinkled with flour. Cover with a plastic wrap and set aside to side for 1-2 hours.

Step 4: Transfer the dough into lightly floured surface. Deflate and knead the dough with hands for 1-2 minutes.

Cut the dough in half. Shape each half into a loaf. Place the loaves into two greased baking trays. Push down with your fingers. Set aside, cover with a plastic wrap and let the dough rise again. This will take approximately one hour.

Step 5: Pre-heat the oven to 365°F. Place the loaf trays into the oven.

Bake at 365° for 40-45 minutes or until it becomes golden brown and baked through.

Transfer onto the cooling racks and let it cool.

Wild Rice Bread will keep for one week in a fridge or up to one month in a freezer.

Whole Wheat Zucchini Bread

INGREDIENTS:

1 ½ Cup Flour, all-purpose

1 ½ Cup Flour, whole wheat

3 Cups Zucchini, grated

2 Eggs, large

1 ¼ Tablespoons Olive oil, cold pressed, unrefined

½ Cup Sugar, brown

½ Cup Molasses

1 Cup Raisins, golden

½ Cup Pecans, chopped

½ Cup Walnuts, chopped

½ Cup Pistachios, chopped

2 teaspoons Salt, fine, sea

1 teaspoon Baking powder

1 teaspoon Vanilla, extract, pure

¼ teaspoon Cinnamon, powder

EQUIPMENT:

Large and medium mixing bowls, Grater, Whisk, Spatula, Two loaf baking trays, Cooling racks.

PREPARATION:

Step 1: Preheat the oven to 355°F. Grease the loaf baking trays. Drain the excess water from zucchinis.

Step 2: In a medium mixing bowl combine all dry ingredients: flour, wheat flour, sugar, pecans, walnuts, pistachios, cranberries, raisins, salt, baking powder and cinnamon. Whisk together.

Step 3: In a large mixing bowl combine all wet ingredients: zucchinis, molasses, eggs, olive oil, and vanilla. Whisk together.

Step 4: Combine dry and wet ingredients in the large bowl. Fold in with a spatula to incorporate all together.

Step 5: Distribute the batter between two greased trays. Bake for 45-50 minutes at 355°F or until the wooden tester comes out clean.

Transfer onto the cooling racks and let it cool.

Whole Wheat Zucchini Bread will keep for one week in a fridge or up to one month in a freezer.

Dates & Nuts Bread

INGREDIENTS:

2 Cups Flour, all-purpose

2 Cups Dates, chopped

¾ Cup Water, warm

½ Cup Cocoa, powder, unsweetened

2 Eggs, large

2 Tablespoons Olive oil, cold pressed, unrefined

2 Tablespoons Butter, softened

1 Cup Molasses

½ Cup Sugar, brown

½ Cup Macadamia nuts, chopped

½ Cup Walnuts, chopped

½ Cup Hazelnuts, chopped

1 Tablespoon Brandy

2 teaspoons Salt, fine, sea

1 teaspoon Baking powder

1 teaspoon Vanilla, extract, pure

EQUIPMENT:

Large and medium mixing bowls, Whisk, Spatula, Two loaf baking trays, Cooling racks.

PREPARATION:

Step 1: Preheat the oven to 355°F. Grease the loaf baking trays.

Step 2: In a medium mixing bowl combine all dry ingredients: flour, brown sugar, cocoa powder, dates, macadamia nuts, walnuts, hazelnuts, salt, and baking powder. Whisk together.

Step 3: In a large mixing bowl combine all wet ingredients: water, molasses, eggs, olive oil, and butter. Whisk together.

Step 4: Combine dry and wet ingredients in the large bowl. Add vanilla extract and brandy. Fold in with a spatula to incorporate all together.

Step 5: Distribute the batter between two greased trays. Bake for 45-50 minutes at 355°F or until the wooden tester comes out clean.

Transfer onto the cooling racks and let it cool.

Dates & Nuts Bread will keep for one week in a fridge or up to one month in a freezer.

Mushrooms Bread

INGREDIENTS:

3 Cups Flour, all-purpose

4 Cups Mushrooms, white, coarsely chopped

2 Cups Onions, yellow, chopped

2 Tablespoons Butter, unsalted

2 Eggs, large

½ Cup Water, warm

2 ¼ Tablespoons Olive oil, cold pressed, unrefined

½ Tablespoon Sugar, brown

2 teaspoons Salt, fine, sea

1 teaspoon Baking powder

1 teaspoon Vanilla, extract, pure

¼ teaspoon Nutmeg, powder

¼ teaspoon Black pepper, powder

EQUIPMENT:

Medium skillet, Large, medium, and small mixing bowls, Grater, Whisk, Spatula, Two loaf baking trays, Cooling racks.

PREPARATION:

Step 1: Add butter into a skillet and heat it over medium heat. Place mushrooms and onions into the skillet. Fry it on medium heat for 5-7 minutes until mushrooms become fragrant. Set aside.

Step 2: Preheat the oven to 355°F. Grease the loaf baking trays.

Step 3: In a medium mixing bowl combine all dry ingredients: flour, sugar, salt, baking powder, nutmeg, and black pepper. Whisk together.

Step 4: In a large mixing bowl combine all wet ingredients: water, mushrooms, eggs, olive oil, and vanilla. Whisk together.

Step 5: Combine dry and wet ingredients in the large bowl. Fold in with a spatula to incorporate all together. If the mixture is too dry add a little bit more water.

Step 6: Distribute the batter between two greased trays. Bake for 45-50 minutes at 355°F or until the wooden tester comes out clean.

Transfer onto the cooling racks and let it cool.

Mushroom Bread will keep for one week in a fridge or up to one month in a freezer.

Potato Mushroom Bread

INGREDIENTS:

5 Cups Flour, all-purpose

6 Oz Potato, boiled

6 Oz Mushrooms, white chopped

2 Tablespoons Butter, unsalted

2 ½ Cup Milk, warm

2 ¼ Tablespoons Olive oil, cold pressed, unrefined

1 ½ teaspoons Sugar, cane, white

1 ¼ tablespoon Yeast, dry, active

2 teaspoons Salt, fine, sea

EQUIPMENT:

Medium skillet, Stand mixer fitted with the dough hook, Small and medium mixing bowls, Potato masher, Whisk, Plastic wrap. Two loaf baking trays, Cooling racks.

PREPARATION:

Step 1: Add butter into a skillet and heat it over medium heat. Place mushrooms into the skillet. Fry it on medium heat for 5-7 minutes until mushrooms become fragrant. Set aside.

Step 2: In a small mixing bowl add dry yeast and two tablespoons of warm milk. Set aside on a countertop for 3-5 minutes to foam.

Remove skin from the boiled potato. Place the skinned potato into a medium mixing bowl and mash with a masher. Whisk in warm milk.

Add salt, yeast, olive oil, and sugar. Whisk to incorporate.

Whisk in two cups of flour.

Step 3: Transfer the mixture into the bowl of a stand mixer. Start mixing on medium-low speed and slowly add the rest of the flour. If the dough is sticking to the sides of the bowl, scrape it with a spatula. The dough will soon start forming a sturdy but soft ball.

Step 4: Leave the dough in the bowl, cover with a plastic wrap and set aside in a warm place for approximately two hours. The dough should at least double in size.

Step 5: Transfer the dough into lightly floured surface. Knead the dough with hands for 1-2 minutes. Fold in mushrooms.

Cut the dough in half. Shape each half into a loaf. Place the loaves into two greased baking trays. Push down with your fingers. Set aside, cover with a plastic wrap and let the dough rise again.

Step 6: Pre-heat the oven to 350°F. Place the loaf trays into the oven.

Bake at 350° for 30-35 minutes or until it becomes golden brown and baked through.

Transfer onto the cooling racks and let it cool.

Potato Mushroom Bread will keep for one week in a fridge or up to one month in a freezer.

Olive Bread

INGREDIENTS:

4 Cups Flour, all-purpose

1 ¾ Cup Olives, black, pitted

1 ¼ Cup Water, warm

2 ¼ Tablespoons Olive oil, cold pressed, unrefined

1 ½ teaspoons Sugar, cane, white

3/4 Tablespoon Yeast, dry, active

2 teaspoons Salt, fine, sea

1 teaspoon Rosemary, dried

EQUIPMENT:

Stand mixer fitted with the dough hook, Medium and large mixing bowls, Two baking trays, Parchment paper, Cooling racks, Plastic wrap (optional).

PREPARATION:

Step 1: In a large mixing bowl, combine flour, olives, yeast, herbs, and salt. Mix with a spatula to combine. Add water, olive oil and mix with the spatula to incorporate. Cover the bowl with a plastic wrap and set aside at room temperature for 1-2 hours to rise.

Step 2: After the dough has risen, transfer it onto work surface dusted with flour. Knead the dough for 1-2 minutes, fold the dough in half, and then roll it into a ball.

Step 3: Generously sprinkle the bottom of a medium mixing bowl with flour. Place the dough ball into the mixing bowl and cover it with a plastic wrap. Set it aside for two hour to rise.

Step 4: Transfer the dough into a lightly floured surface. Knead it with hands for 1-2 minutes. Cut the dough in half. Shape each half into a loaf.

Step 5: Pre-heat the oven to 375°F. Line the baking trays with parchment paper. Place the loaves into the baking trays.

Bake at 375° for 30-35 minutes or until it becomes golden brown and baked through.

Transfer onto the cooling racks and let it cool.

Olive Bread will keep for one week in a fridge or up to one month in a freezer.

Strawberry Nut Bread

INGREDIENTS:

2 Cups Flour, all-purpose

2 Cups Strawberries, chopped

¾ Cup Water, warm

2 Eggs, large

2 Tablespoons Olive oil, cold pressed, unrefined

2 Tablespoons Butter, softened

1 Cup Molasses

½ Cup Sugar, brown

½ Cup Macadamia nuts, chopped

½ Cup Walnuts, chopped

2 teaspoons Salt, fine, sea

1 teaspoon Baking powder

1 teaspoon Vanilla, extract, pure

EQUIPMENT:

Large and medium mixing bowls, Grater, Whisk, Spatula, Two loaf baking trays, Cooling racks.

PREPARATION:

Step 1: Preheat the oven to 355°F. Grease the loaf baking trays.

Step 2: In a medium mixing bowl combine all dry ingredients: flour, brown sugar, macadamia nuts, walnuts, salt, and baking powder. Whisk together.

Step 3: In a large mixing bowl combine all wet ingredients: strawberries, water, molasses, eggs, olive oil, and butter. Whisk together.

Step 4: Combine dry and wet ingredients in the large bowl. Add vanilla extract. Fold in the ingredients with a spatula to incorporate all together.

Step 5: Distribute the batter between two greased trays. Bake for 45-50 minutes at 355°F or until the wooden tester comes out clean.

Transfer onto the cooling racks and let it cool.

Strawberry Nut Bread will keep for one week in a fridge or up to one month in a freezer.

Plum Bread

INGREDIENTS:

2 Cups Flour, all-purpose

2 Cups Plums, dried, pitted, chopped

1 Cup Raisins, brown

1 Cup Walnuts, chopped

¾ Cup Water, warm

2 Eggs, large

2 ½ Tablespoons Olive oil, cold pressed, unrefined

1 Cup Molasses

½ Cup Sugar, brown

2 teaspoons Salt, fine, sea

1 teaspoon Baking powder

1 teaspoon Vanilla, extract, pure

¼ teaspoon Nutmeg, powder

EQUIPMENT:

Large and medium mixing bowls, Grater, Whisk, Spatula, Two loaf baking trays, Cooling racks.

PREPARATION:

Step 1: Preheat the oven to 355°F. Grease the loaf baking trays.

Step 2: In a medium mixing bowl combine all dry ingredients: flour, brown sugar, plums, raisins, walnuts, salt, and baking powder. Whisk together.

Step 3: In a large mixing bowl combine all wet ingredients: water, molasses, eggs, and olive oil. Whisk together.

Step 4: Combine dry and wet ingredients in the large bowl. Add vanilla extract. Fold in the ingredients with a spatula to incorporate all together.

Step 5: Distribute the batter between two greased trays. Bake for 45-50 minutes at 355°F or until the wooden tester comes out clean.

Transfer onto the cooling racks and let it cool.

Plum Bread will keep for one week in a fridge or up to one month in a freezer.

Banana Nut Bread

INGREDIENTS:

3 Cups Flour, all-purpose

5 Bananas, mashed

2 Eggs, large

2 ¼ Tablespoons Olive oil, cold pressed, unrefined

1 ½ Cup Sugar, brown

1 Cup Pecans, chopped

1 Cup Walnuts, chopped

1 Cup Cranberries, dried

2 teaspoons Salt, fine, sea

1 teaspoon Baking powder

1 teaspoon Vanilla, extract, pure

EQUIPMENT:

Large and medium mixing bowls, Masher, Whisk, Spatula, Two loaf baking trays, Cooling racks.

PREPARATION:

Step 1: Preheat the oven to 355°F. Grease the loaf baking trays. Mash bananas with a masher.

Step 2: In a medium mixing bowl combine all dry ingredients: flour, brown sugar, pecans, walnuts, cranberries, salt, and baking powder. Whisk together.

Step 3: In a large mixing bowl combine all wet ingredients: bananas, eggs, olive oil, and vanilla. Whisk together.

Step 4: Combine dry and wet ingredients in the large bowl. Fold in with a spatula to incorporate all together.

Step 5: Distribute the batter between two greased trays. Bake for 50 - 55 minutes at 355°F or until the wooden tester comes out clean.

Transfer onto the cooling racks and let it cool.

Banana Nut Bread will keep for one week in a fridge or up to one month in a freezer.

Banana Chocolate Chip Bread

INGREDIENTS:

3 Cups Flour, all-purpose

5 Bananas, mashed

2 Eggs, large

2 ¼ Tablespoons Olive oil, cold pressed, unrefined

1 ½ Cup Sugar, brown

1 Cup Pecans, chopped

1 Cup Chocolate chips, dark, mini, bakers

2 teaspoons Salt, fine, sea

1 teaspoon Baking powder

1 teaspoon Vanilla, extract, pure

¼ teaspoon Nutmeg, powder

EQUIPMENT:

Large and medium mixing bowls, Masher, Whisk, Spatula, Two loaf baking trays, Cooling racks.

PREPARATION:

Step 1: Preheat the oven to 355°F. Grease the loaf baking trays. Mash bananas with a masher.

Step 2: In a medium mixing bowl combine all dry ingredients: flour, brown sugar, pecans, chocolate chips, salt, baking powder, and nutmeg. Whisk together.

Step 3: In a large mixing bowl combine all wet ingredients: bananas, eggs, olive oil, and vanilla. Whisk together.

Step 4: Combine dry and wet ingredients in the large bowl. Fold in with a spatula to incorporate all together.

Step 5: Distribute the batter between two greased trays. Bake for 50 - 55 minutes at 355°F or until the wooden tester comes out clean.

Transfer onto the cooling racks and let it cool.

Banana Chocolate Chip Bread will keep for one week in a fridge or up to one month in a freezer.

Blueberry Crumble Bread

INGREDIENTS:

FOR THE CRUMBLES:

1 Cup Flour, all purpose

1 Cup Sugar, granulated

3 Oz Butter, unsalted

½ teaspoon Salt, sea, fine

FOR THE BREAD:

3 Cups Flour, all-purpose

3 Cups Blueberries, fresh

2 Eggs, large

1 Cup Milk, whole

2 ¼ Tablespoons Olive oil, cold pressed, unrefined

1 ½ Cup Sugar, cane, white

2 teaspoons Salt, fine, sea

1 teaspoon Baking powder

1 teaspoon Vanilla, extract, pure

EQUIPMENT:

One large and two medium mixing bowls, Whisk, Spatula, Two loaf baking trays, Cooling racks.

PREPARATION:

MAKE THE CRUMBLES:

In a medium bowl, combine flour, sugar and butter. Do not over mix. The mixture will be granular.

MAKE THE BREAD BATTER:

Step 1: Preheat the oven to 355°F. Grease the loaf baking trays.

Step 2: In a medium mixing bowl combine all dry ingredients: flour, sugar, salt, baking powder. Whisk together.

Step 3: In a large mixing bowl combine all wet ingredients: milk, eggs, olive oil, and vanilla. Whisk together.

Step 4: Combine dry and wet ingredients in the large bowl. Fold in with a spatula to incorporate all together. Carefully fold in blueberries.

Step 5: Distribute the batter between two greased trays. Spread the crumbles on top of the bread batter.

Bake for 45-50 minutes at 355°F or until the wooden tester comes out clean.

Transfer onto the cooling racks and let it cool.

Blueberry Crumble Bread will keep for one week in a fridge or up to one month in a freezer.

Carrot Walnut Bread

INGREDIENTS:

3 Cups Flour, all-purpose

3 Cups Carrots, grated

2 Eggs, large

2 ¼ Tablespoons Olive oil, cold pressed, unrefined

2 Cups Molasses

1 Cup Walnuts, chopped

1 Cup Cranberries, dried

2 teaspoons Salt, fine, sea

1 teaspoon Baking powder

1 teaspoon Vanilla, extract, pure

¼ teaspoon Ginger, powder

¼ teaspoon Nutmeg, powder

EQUIPMENT:

Grater, Large, medium, and small mixing bowls, Grater, Whisk, Spatula, Two loaf baking trays, Cooling racks.

PREPARATION:

Step 1: Grate carrots into a small bowl. Set aside.

Step 2: Preheat the oven to 355°F. Grease the loaf baking trays.

Step 3: In a medium mixing bowl combine all dry ingredients: flour, walnuts, cranberry, salt, baking powder, nutmeg, and ginger. Whisk together.

Step 4: In a large mixing bowl combine all wet ingredients: carrots, molasses, eggs, olive oil, and vanilla. Whisk together.

Step 5: Combine dry and wet ingredients in the large bowl. Fold in with a spatula to incorporate all together.

Step 6: Distribute the batter between two greased trays. Bake for 45-50 minutes at 355°F or until the wooden tester comes out clean.

Transfer onto the cooling racks and let it cool.

Carrot Walnut Bread will keep for one week in a fridge or up to one month in a freezer.

Almond Flour Banana Bread

INGREDIENTS:

3 cups Almond Flour

2 Bananas, ripe, mashed

½ cup Almond Milk

¼ cup Honey, raw

¼ cup Olive Oil, virgin, first cold pressed

4 tablespoons Water, hot

2 tablespoons Flax Seeds, ground

1 teaspoon Baking Soda

1 teaspoon Vanilla, extract, pure

¼ teaspoon Salt, fine, pink, Himalayan

Cooking Spray for greasing the baking tray

EQUIPMENT:

Rectangular bread baking tray, Stand or hand mixer fitted with the paddle attachment, Measuring cups, Cup, Fork, Wire cooling racks, Parchment paper (optional), Cake decorating piping tips and bags (optional).

PREPARATION:

Step 1: Prepare egg replacement: add flax seeds into a cup and cover it with hot water. Place flax seeds onto a countertop and wait until flax seeds become gelatin-like.

Step 2: Grease the bottom and sides of the baking tray with a cooking spray. Line the bottom of the tray with parchment paper (optional).

Step 3: In a bowl of a stand mixer, mash bananas with a fork. Add flax eggs, almond flour, almond milk, olive oil, honey, baking soda, salt, and vanilla extract. Process everything on low-medium speed until all is combined.

Step 4: Pour the batter into the baking tray. Bake for about 40 minutes or until a wooden skewer comes out clean.

Step 5: Place on a cooling rack and let it cool for an hour. Decorate with decorating tools before serving. **(Optional)**

Almond Flour Banana Bread will keep for a week in a fridge or one month in a freezer.

Almond Flour Coconut Bread

INGREDIENTS:

2 cups Almond Flour

1 cups Coconut Flour

1 cup Apple Puree

½ cup Almond Milk

¼ cup Honey, raw

¼ cup Olive Oil, virgin, first cold pressed

4 tablespoons Water, hot

2 tablespoons Flax Seeds, ground

1 teaspoon Baking Soda

1 teaspoon Vanilla, extract, pure

¼ teaspoon Salt, fine, pink, Himalayan

Cooking Spray for greasing the baking tray

EQUIPMENT:

Rectangular bread baking tray, Stand or hand mixer fitted with the paddle attachment, Measuring cups, Cup, Fork, Wire cooling racks, Parchment paper (optional), Cake decorating piping tips and bags (optional).

PREPARATION:

Step 1: Prepare egg replacement: add flax seeds into a cup and cover it with hot water. Place flax seeds onto a countertop and wait until flax seeds become gelatin-like.

Step 2: Grease the bottom and sides of the baking tray with a cooking spray. Line the bottom of the tray with parchment paper (optional).

Step 3: In a bowl of a stand mixer add apple puree, flax eggs, almond flour, coconut flour, almond milk, olive oil, honey, baking soda, salt, and vanilla extract. Process everything on low-medium speed until all is combined.

Step 4: Pour the batter into the baking tray. Bake for about 40 minutes or until a wooden skewer comes out clean.

Step 5: Place on a cooling rack and let it cool for an hour. Decorate with decorating tools before serving. **(Optional)**

Almond Flour Coconut Bread will keep for a week in a fridge or one month in a freezer.

Almond Flour Pumpkin Bread

INGREDIENTS:
2 cups Almond Flour
½ cup Coconut Flour
1 cup Pumpkin, puree
½ cup Almond Milk
¼ cup Honey, raw
¼ cup Olive Oil, virgin, first cold pressed
4 tablespoons Water, hot
2 tablespoons Flax Seeds, ground
1 teaspoon Baking Soda
1 teaspoon Vanilla, extract, pure
½ teaspoon Pumpkin Pie Spice
½ teaspoon Cinnamon, powder
¼ teaspoon Salt, fine, pink, Himalayan
Cooking Spray for greasing the baking tray
EQUIPMENT:

Rectangular bread baking tray, Stand or hand mixer fitted with the paddle attachment, Measuring cups, Cup, Fork, Wire cooling racks, Parchment paper (optional), Cake decorating piping tips and bags (optional).

PREPARATION:

Preheat the oven to 365°F.

Step 1: Cut the raw pumpkin, remove the seeds.

Place pumpkin pieces onto a baking tray. Bake the pumpkin for approximately forty minutes until it is soft. Set aside to cool. Place cooled pumpkin into the food processor. Process until smooth. Set aside.

Step 2: Prepare egg replacement: add flax seeds into a cup and cover it with hot water. Place flax seeds onto a countertop and wait until flax seeds become gelatin-like.

Alternatively, you can use 3-4 eggs.

Step 3: Preheat the oven to 355°F. Grease bottom and sides of the baking tray with a cooking spray. Line the bottom of the tray with parchment paper (optional).

Step 4: In a bowl add flax eggs, pumpkin puree, almond flour, coconut flour, almond milk, honey, olive oil, baking soda, salt, and spices. Process everything on low-medium speed until all is combined.

Step 5: Pour the batter into the baking tray. Bake for about 40 minutes or until a wooden skewer comes out clean.

Step 6: Place on a cooling rack and let it cool for an hour. Decorate with decorating tools before serving. **(Optional)**

Banana Flour Pumpkin Bread will keep for a week in a fridge or one month in a freezer.

Coconut Flour Banana Bread

INGREDIENTS:

3 cups Coconut Flour

2 Bananas, ripe, mashed

3 cups Coconut Milk

¼ cup Honey, raw

¼ cup Olive Oil, virgin, first cold pressed

1 teaspoon Baking Soda

1 teaspoon Vanilla, extract, pure

¼ teaspoon Salt, fine, pink, Himalayan

Cooking Spray for greasing the baking tray

For Flaxseed Egg:

4 tablespoons Water, hot

2 tablespoons Flax Seeds, ground

EQUIPMENT:

Rectangular bread baking tray, Stand or hand mixer fitted with the paddle attachment, Measuring cups, Cup, Fork, Wire cooling racks, Parchment paper (optional), Cake decorating piping tips and bags (optional).

PREPARATION:

Step 1: Prepare egg replacement: add flax seeds into a cup and cover it with hot water. Place flax seeds onto a countertop and wait until flax seeds become gelatin-like.

Step 2: Preheat the oven to 355°F. With a cooking spray grease the bottom and sides of the baking tray. Line the bottoms of the tray with parchment paper (optional).

Step 3: In a bowl of a stand mixer, mash bananas with a fork. Add flax eggs, coconut flour, olive oil, coconut milk, honey, baking soda, salt, and vanilla extract. Process everything on low-medium speed until all is combined.

Step 4: Pour the batter into the baking tray. Bake for about 40 minutes or until a wooden skewer comes out clean.

Step 5: Place on a cooling rack and let it cool for an hour. Decorate with decorating tools before serving. **(Optional)**

Coconut Flour Banana Bread will keep for a week in a fridge or one month in a freezer.

Coconut Flour Pumpkin Bread

INGREDIENTS:

2 cups Coconut Flour

1 ¾ cups Coconut Milk

½ cup Coconut Flour

1 cup Pumpkin, puree

¼ cup Honey, raw

¼ cup Olive Oil, virgin, first cold pressed

1 teaspoon Baking Soda

1 teaspoon Vanilla, extract, pure

½ teaspoon Pumpkin Pie Spice

½ teaspoon Cinnamon, powder

¼ teaspoon Salt, fine, pink, Himalayan

For Flaxseed Egg:

4 tablespoons Water, hot

2 tablespoons Flax Seeds, ground

Cooking Spray for greasing the baking tray

EQUIPMENT:

Rectangular bread baking tray, Stand or hand mixer fitted with the paddle attachment, Measuring cups, Cup, Fork, Wire cooling racks, Parchment paper (optional), Cake decorating piping tips and bags (optional).

PREPARATION:

Preheat the oven to 365°F.

Step 1: Cut pumpkin in half and remove the seeds. Cut pumpkin on pieces. Spray the baking tray with a cooking spray. Place pumpkin pieces onto the baking tray. Bake for approximately 40 minutes until pumpkin becomes soft. Set aside to cool.

Step 2: Place cooled pumpkin into the food processor. Process until smooth. Set aside.

Step 3: Prepare egg replacement: add flax seeds into a cup and cover it with hot water. Place flax seeds onto a countertop and wait until flax seeds become gelatin-like.

Alternatively, you can use 3-4 eggs.

Step 4: Preheat the oven to 355°F. Grease the bottom and sides of the baking tray with the cooking spray. Line the bottom of the tray with parchment paper (optional).

Step 5: In a bowl of stand mixer equipped with the paddle attachment add flax eggs, pumpkin puree, coconut flour, coconut flour, coconut milk, honey, baking soda, salt, and spices. Process everything on low-medium speed until all is combined.

Step 6: Pour the batter into the bread baking tray. Bake for about 40 minutes or until a wooden skewer comes out clean.

Step 7: Place on a cooling rack and let it cool for an hour. Decorate with decorating tools before serving. **(Optional)**

www.ingramcontent.com/pod-product-compliance
Lightning Source LLC
Chambersburg PA
CBHW071453070526
44578CB00001B/323